P9-CCA-395

Capsize!

Written by Susan Griffiths
Illustrated by Graeme Tavendale

Contents   Page

Rigby

Capsize!

With this character ...

Judy
Folson

"She wa

Setting the scene ...

Deep in the icy, cold southern Indian Ocean, a lone sailor is sailing through a fierce storm. She's in the lead in an around-the-world yacht race, which means that she is a long way from help if something disastrous happens. What she *doesn't* know is that the weather is about to get a lot worse . . . and the southern Indian Ocean is about to become a very lonely place. She fights to keep her small yacht afloat—but just when the storm seems to have calmed down, disaster strikes!

eeling desperate—and very, very lonely."

Chapter 1

"Just keep calm, Judy. Just keep calm."

Judy Folson was talking to herself. She was worried. Huge green waves crashed against her tiny yacht, the *Starling*. Far away in the distance, Judy spotted icebergs. The wind was freezing and wet on her face.

The *Starling* rolled wildly in the
rough sea, and Judy groaned as she
fell to one side. She wore safety straps
to stop her from being washed
overboard . . . but she also held on
tight to the large wheel that steered her
boat. She knew she had to keep the
yacht heading straight into the waves.
If one of the waves hit her sideways,
the *Starling* might roll over. Capsizing
in this storm would be a disaster!

"Just keep calm. This storm can't
last forever!" she said to herself.

Judy was sailing the *Starling* around the world single-handedly. She had been sailing yachts for many years but had never been on such a long, hard journey by herself. However, competing in a famous around-the-world yacht race was an adventure too good to miss. As soon as she had heard about it, she had entered.

After months of preparation and training, she had lined up at the starting line off the coast of England with twenty other small yachts. A cannon had boomed from the deck of a huge navy ship—and the race had begun.

That had been five weeks ago. To Judy, in the middle of the storm, it seemed like five years ago! She had sailed from England to Portugal. From Portugal, she had sailed down the west coast of Africa to Cape Town. From Cape Town, she had sailed around the Cape of Good Hope and eastward into the Indian Ocean.

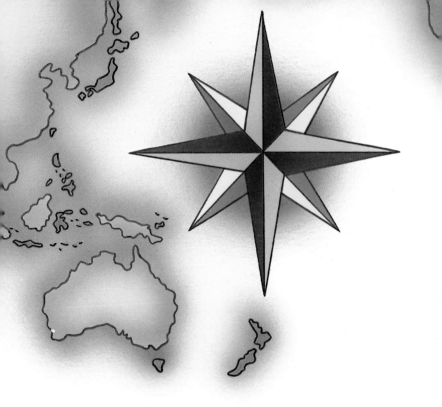

In the southern Indian Ocean, strong winds pushed her eastward. Now she was a long way south, where the winds were strongest. She was making good time toward her next stop: Perth, Australia.

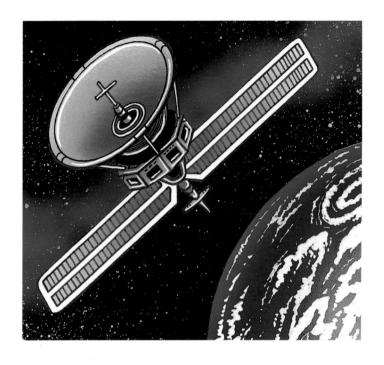

After Judy spent hours fighting the storm, the wind died down and the waves became smaller. Exhausted, Judy untied her safety straps. She went below deck to drink something warm. As far as she knew, she was leading in the around-the-world yacht race. But she still had a long way to sail on her journey.

Below the deck, she wondered what Bob was doing. Bob was a weather forecaster, thousands of miles away, in a small town in the United States. Judy had never met him, but each morning he transmitted his forecasts to all the yachts in the race. Bob received weather information from many satellites and weather stations around the world. He combined all the information and sent forecasts every twelve hours using a telecommunications satellite.

Judy relied on Bob to tell her what weather to expect. The weather forecast that she had received on her small computer last night had not looked good. The weather in Judy's remote part of the world was getting worse.

Thousands of miles away in London, the race organizers waited for each of the yachts to check in by radio. If a race competitor did not check in at least once a day, they started to worry. The leading boats were in the southern Indian Ocean. That was a long way from the nearest help, so the race organizers were relieved each time they received a message from a yacht. They figured that Judy's yacht was still a week's sailing time away from Perth.

Below the deck, Judy waited for her small electric teakettle to boil. The roaring wind had kept her batteries fully charged for the last few days, so she was not worried about power. But she did want to make it to Australia as quickly as she could. She was low on food and had only a few quarts of fresh water left.

She had just poured boiling water over the powdered soup in her cup, when she felt her stomach rise. It was like falling backward on a swing. She felt the floor beneath her feet drop down. At the same time, her head cracked against the roof of the cabin. She knew immediately what had happened.

The yacht had fallen into a huge trough between two massive waves. She felt a sudden stab of fear. Was the boat side alongside, or facing the huge wave?

Suddenly, Judy felt as if she was in a huge cement mixer. Everything around her flew wildly about the cabin, and she crashed heavily against the door.

Judy tried to hold on to one of the railings around the cabin, but her arm and wrist were twisted as the cabin rocked from side to side. In a flash, everything was dark, and there was a loud, cracking noise above her.

She could see nothing in the darkness. When she finally managed to stand upright, she knew she was in a lot of trouble. She was already up to her knees in freezing seawater. And the roof of the cabin was now the floor. The *Starling* had been capsized by the massive waves!

Chapter 2.

Gradually, Judy's eyes became used to the dark. It was still daylight outside, and some light filtered through the gray, cold water into the cabin.

Her first task was to climb out of the icy water. She managed to lift herself onto the upside-down edge of the bunk. Then she looked around the wrecked cabin.

The water had damaged all the electrical equipment that Judy needed to communicate with the race organizers in London. Her radio, her fax machine, and her satellite tracking device were all ruined. What was worse, the galley, where she kept all her food, was completely underwater.

She spotted her plastic bottles of fresh water bobbing in the seawater at her feet and grabbed one of them. Fresh water was vital for survival.

She wasn't due to check in with the race organizers for another twelve hours. So she knew she would have to try to survive for much longer than that before she was rescued—*if* she was rescued. Although she didn't know it, Bob had just sent a severe storm warning informing all boats to stay away from the area where Judy had capsized.

Judy knew that by the time a rescue alert was made, she would have drifted far away from her last check-in position. The strong, fast currents in this part of the ocean would carry her quickly away from her last known position. The *Starling* would be very difficult to find. She was feeling desperate—and very, very lonely.

Suddenly, Judy remembered her emergency radio beacon, safely tucked away deep within the hull of the *Starling.* It was her only hope of being rescued, but for that to work, someone had to be looking for her. The radio beacon was not powerful enough to be detected unless you were within a few hundred miles. At that moment, Judy felt that this was probably the most isolated place on earth. And it was a cold, wet, place, with no food. Her situation was looking worse as time slipped by.

Chapter 3.

Judy didn't sleep at all that night. Cramped in the tiny upside-down cabin of the *Starling*, she wondered when the race organizers in London would realize something was wrong. She was wet, cold, and very hungry. Judy liked an adventure—but right now, she would give anything to be safely tucked up in a warm bed on dry land.

"Just keep calm, Judy," she said to herself again and again. "If they don't hear from me soon, they'll realize that something terrible has happened."

If Judy had been able to see out of her cabin, she would have seen a tiny line of light in the distance. It was a huge container ship, the *Magellan*, plowing through the high, heavy seas. If she had been able to let off a bright red flare, the ship might have turned and rescued her.

But the captain of the *Magellan* had no idea that, barely five miles away, a lone sailor was in desperate need of his help. The line of light grew dimmer and dimmer as the *Magellan* sailed into the distance.

While Judy sat huddled in her cabin, the race organizers in London were having an emergency meeting. No communication had been received from the *Starling* for a long time.

"It's time to start a rescue plan," said one of the organizers, looking at a map of the Indian Ocean. "It's time to contact the Australians."

Judy had never felt so cold. Although she had a bottle of fresh water to sip, it had been two days since she had eaten anything. It felt as if her bones were made of ice. Judy tried to keep warm, but the temperature in the cabin had dropped close to the freezing point. Fortunately, the yacht was being kept afloat by the air bubble trapped under the hull in the cabin.

But she also knew that it would take only one more huge wave to tip the *Starling* over and fill it with freezing water. There would be no second chance if that happened. She would drown.

Chapter 4.

As Judy shivered and waited, navigation experts in Australia huddled over a map of the Indian Ocean, trying to figure out where the *Starling* might be located. They could estimate the speed and direction of the winds that might be carrying the small yacht eastward. They could also estimate how far off course the strong currents might have pushed the yacht.

They chose an area that was the most likely spot to start looking and called the air force. They needed to get an airplane into the area fast to start searching.

Finally . . . the breakthrough that people around the world had been waiting for. After hours of searching, the airplane's radio operator heard a distress signal from the *Starling*'s emergency radio beacon. He quickly figured out where the signal was coming from and informed the pilot of the airplane. The airplane swung around and headed in a southeasterly direction.

The current had pushed Judy a lot farther off course than they had thought. The radio operator radioed the news to Perth. A few minutes later, the race organizers in London excitedly waited for the next news update. At least the yacht might be found. But was Judy still alive?

The airplane reported no sign of a life raft. All they spotted was the overturned hull of the badly damaged *Starling*. They could not tell if Judy had survived those three long, cold days.

Chapter 5.

Judy was extremely cold and hungry. She knew that hypothermia was a very dangerous condition, so she tried to avoid it by moving her arms and legs to keep warm. But the icy water had soaked everything, and her bones felt frozen.

She also knew that hypothermia could make you think in strange ways, so she was frightened when she found herself imagining a low thudding noise coming through the hull. What could it be? She decided that she was just imagining it and tried to keep the blood flowing in her body by rubbing her arms and legs.

The noise was coming from the
engines of the *Magellan*. The captain
of the container ship had turned back
toward the *Starling* the moment he
had received the radio message.
The air force airplane had spotted the
Magellan on its way back to base
and had requested its help.

Judy wondered if she was imagining the strange sounds again. Then she realized what the sound was! Tired and feeling as if she was in a dream, she swung into action. She reached down into the murky water and pulled open the cabin hatch. Holding her breath, she lowered herself into the icy water and blindly pulled herself up along the side of the yacht. After what seemed like ages, she finally surfaced. She struggled onto the hull of the *Starling* and turned her head. A giant ship rose out of the waves! Two sailors in a small, yellow inflatable raft were speeding toward her. It was the best sight that Judy had ever seen!

The return trip to the *Magellan* was fast. Judy was quickly wrapped up, from head to toe, in shiny aluminum foil to conserve what little body heat she had left. She sipped some hot, sweet tea from a thermos. She lay back and drifted in and out of consciousness. She wasn't even aware of being winched up onto the deck of the *Magellan.*

She was safe. And although her part in the race was over, she didn't care. She was alive. And . . . she was *still* going to be the first of the around-the-world sailors to arrive in Australia!

"Just keep calm."

Thunderous seas, big waves crashing,
Against an upturned yacht they're smashing.
Hopelessly lost, cold to the bone,
A person waits, entirely alone.

Her yacht capsized in water cold,
And a rescue drama did unfold.
Alone and trapped inside the boat,
It's a race against time to stay afloat.